In a
Lick
 of a Flick
 of a
Tongue

In a Lick of a Flick of a Tongue

Linda Hirschmann
Illustrated by Jeni Bassett

DODD, MEAD & COMPANY   New York

1 2 3 4 5 6 7 8 9 10

Library of Congress Cataloging in Publication Data

Hirschmann. Linda.
    In a lick of a flick of a tongue.

    SUMMARY: Describes the tongues of various
animals and the ways they are used.
    1. Tongue – Juvenile literature. [1. Tongue]
I. Bassett, Jeni. II. Title.
QL946.H58   591.4'3   80-12632
ISBN 0-396-07833-8

With thanks to my BCL, Leah, who introduced me to a blue butterfly and a nuevo mundo as well – L.H.

To Louise M. Tooke – J.B.

In a
Lick
of a Flick
of a
Tongue

Without your tongue to shove, slide, flick, and flutter
How would you clean your teeth of peanut butter?

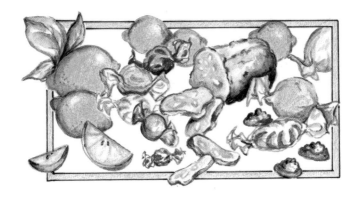

You use your tongue in many ways. If you couldn't lick with your tongue, you'd have to bite lollipops off their sticks. You would have to eat an ice cream cone with a spoon.

If you couldn't move your tongue, you would not be able to speak clearly. Prove it. Press down on your tongue with your finger. Then say, "Rabbits think ladders reach the rainbow. Every lion laughs on Tuesday." Even *you* can't understand what you say unless you move your tongue when you talk.

Your tongue also helps you taste foods. Many thousands of taste buds cover your tongue. They help you learn if foods are sour, salty, or sweet.

With a lick or a flick of your tongue you can taste or talk. Animals, fish, and birds depend on their tongues, too. They may use their tongues to hunt for food . . . or to clean themselves . . . or even to repair their homes. However a tongue is used, it is a most important tool.

All cats – house cats, tigers, leopards, and lions, too –
Lick and flick. Then they've had both a bath and shampoo.

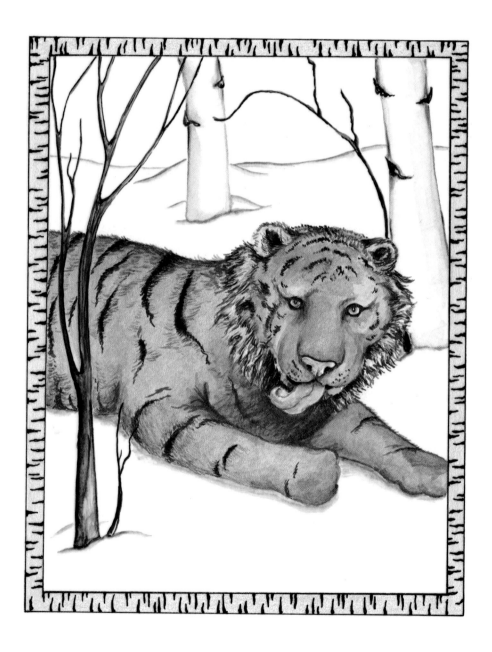

Close-up of
tongue

A cat's tongue is not as smooth as yours. It is covered with
tiny, thorn-like points. When a cat drinks, these thorny
points help it lap up milk or water. They also help a cat keep
clean. When a cat licks itself, its rough tongue combs the dirt
and germs out from its fur.

House cats clean themselves often. Wild cats do also.
They have to. If tigers or lions were dirty, other animals
could smell them more easily. The zebras or deer they were
hunting would sniff the cats and run from the danger. Clean
cats have a better chance to surprise and catch their food
before it gets away.

When you are overheated, you perspire to cool off. But no dog can perspire. Not a pet dog – like a collie or a mutt. Not any of their wild relatives — like a fox or a wolf. When they are overheated, these animals hang out their tongues and pant. The air passing over their tongues and into their throats helps them feel cooler.

A dog uses its tongue to scoop up water from a pond or a bowl. It also uses it to lick a hurt paw. With the saliva on its tongue, the dog cleans and seals its wound.

Licks with its tongue – that's a dog's natural way
To clean up its pup, to greet friends in play.

Quicker than a slingshot,
That's the tongue a frog's got.

Stick out your tongue and try to touch your nose with it. Maybe you can't. That is because your tongue is attached in the back of your mouth and you can stick out only its tip.

A frog sticks out its whole tongue. Its tongue is attached in front, so the frog can flip the back of it up, over, and out of its mouth. It whips out its tongue to catch crickets, ladybugs, and flies. When the tongue hits a bug, it sticks to it. That is because the saliva on a frog's tongue is like glue. It is so sticky that the bug can't get away. Quickly then, the frog flips its tongue and the bug into its mouth. In a gulp the bug's gone.

The insects wiggle but it is no use –
They're stuck, out of luck, and they won't get loose
From the long tongue of a chameleon.

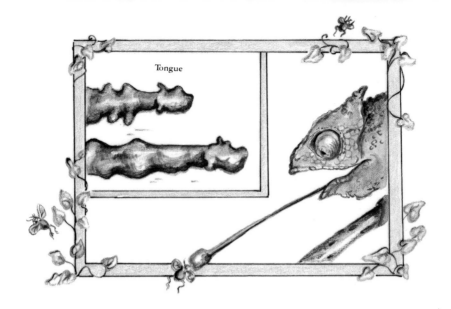

Tongue

Inside the chameleon's tongue is a bone that is surrounded by muscles. Whenever these muscles tighten and squeeze, the bone and tongue shoot from the chameleon's mouth – WHOOSH! – like wet soap can fly from your hand when you squeeze it.

When a chameleon shoots its tongue out in a straight line, it can easily lick up a fly as far as one foot away. But its sticky tongue is so long the chameleon must aim carefully or it could miss food close by. To catch a nearby cricket, it flicks its tongue up, then down in a curve. The club-shaped tip of its tongue hits and sticks to the insect. Its tongue then snaps back into the chameleon's mouth.

Inside its mouth, the chameleon's long tongue folds up like a closed accordion. If it didn't, it wouldn't fit in.

In a flick of its tongue the snake knows
What you learn with your eyes, ears, and nose.

The snake uses its tongue to sense danger and food. Its tongue is forked into two long tips. When a snake's tongue flicks out, its tips lick the air. They touch the ground. Quickly then, the snake flips in its tongue. It shoves the two tips into two holes in the roof of its mouth. These holes "read" the tastes the tongue tips collected. Some tastes warn, "Enemy to the right. Careful!" Other tastes tell the snake where to find a rabbit, frog, or lizard to eat.

No snake's tongue is dangerous but it helps to scare other animals. When a rattlesnake flicks out its tongue, hisses, and rattles, its enemies move far away.

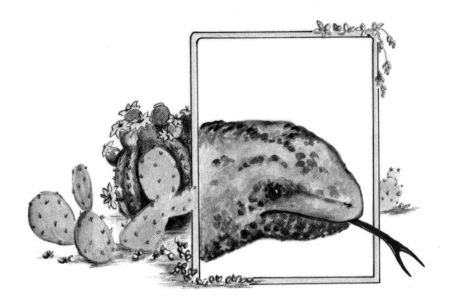

The Gila monster lizard finds food in the same way that snakes do. It flicks its forked tongue out, then back into its mouth and "reads" the tastes in the air.

Gilas live in deserts. To escape the worst heat they sleep for months without waking. This summertime hibernation is called *estivation*. While it estivates, a Gila lives off the food it has stored in its fat tail. When it wakes, its tail is thin and the Gila must eat. Then it flicks out its tongue in search of food.

But a Gila crawls so very slowly it can catch only baby birds, slow-moving insects — and eggs that don't move at all. After eating, it will rest again.

Where will Gila snooze next?
It will choose as it chews.

Like yo-yo strings spin down, up, and down as they whirl,
A butterfly's tongue rolls down, then lifts in a curl.

Can you drink when your mouth is closed? You could if you used a soda straw. A butterfly drinks in almost that way.

The butterfly's "straw" is its tube-like tongue that grows out from its mouth. This tongue is also called a *proboscis*. It is as thin as a thread but the butterfly can drink through it. First, the insect rolls its tongue down into a flower to reach the nectar that lies deep inside it. The butterfly sips that sweet liquid. Then, after drinking, it twirls its tongue up from the blossom and into a tightly curled coil.

The butterfly cannot pull its coiled tongue into its mouth. So instead, it tucks the tongue under its head.

Flying and dining in the darkest of hours,
Bats feed on figs, dates, cactus, cattle, and flowers.

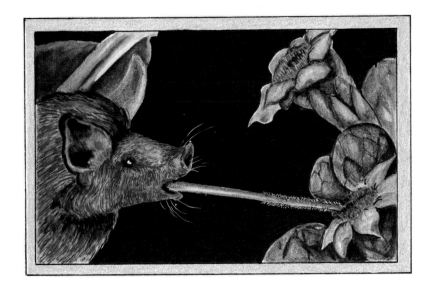

There are hundreds of species of bats. They all eat at night but they don't feed on the same types of food. Their tongues are not alike either.

Fruit bats have long, brush-like tongues. With them they pull out the pulp of mangoes, figs, and dates. They also use their tongues to lick up the fruits' juices.

Vampire bats bite cattle on their necks or backs. Then they form a tube with their tongues and lower lips and feed on the cattle's blood.

Nectar-feeding bats shove their snouts and tongues deep into flowers to lap up the liquid. Since they feed after dark, bats can drink only from night-blooming flowers.

Fuzzy and buzzing, honeybees fly to flowers and dip
Down with their tongues to gather the nectar,
sip by sweet sip.

Tongue

Using its tongue as a tube, the honeybee sips nectar from flowers. It also uses its tongue when it builds and repairs its comb. First the bee licks plants to collect a liquid called resin. Then it flies back to its comb. Flipping its tongue like a paintbrush, the bee covers its walls and floors with the resin to seal up cracks and small holes.

Since bees are small, their tongues are tiny. But compared to its size, a bee's tongue is huge. If the honeybee were as tall as you, its tongue would be as long as you — head to toe. Its tongue is so long that only part of it can fit into the bee's mouth. The rest fits into a groove under its head.

Your arm is as long as the tongue of a giraffe,
If shoulder to wrist measures a foot and a half.

Your tongue can only bend and fold. A giraffe can curl its tongue. It wraps its tongue around a tree branch – just as a monkey wraps a branch with its tail. With its tongue, the giraffe strips off leaves and tender sprouts and shoves this food into its mouth.

Its tongue helps the giraffe stay safe. Giraffes are about 16½ feet (5 meters) tall. To bend down to drink, they must spread their legs so far apart that they are defenseless if an enemy surprises them. But because of their height and extra-long tongues, giraffes need not bend to eat. They can stand tall and watch for danger while they stretch out their tongues and gobble down leaves pulled from trees.

The anteater has no teeth and it doesn't need any. It swallows its food without chewing. An anteater gathers food with flicks of its long, bubble-gum-pink, sticky tongue. It whips its tongue in and out of a small hole in its snout.

The anteater searches for termites in their tall, cement-hard nests and in soft, rotten trees. It claws those nests and trees apart. It hunts ants by poking its snout into anthills.

When it finds food – ZIP! – its tongue shoots from its snout. Its long tongue can even chase ants through their underground tunnels. In one lick that sticky tongue is covered with termites or ants.

Eaten by the snoutful,
It's doubtful
That ants like anteaters.

Peck, pecking, the woodpecker pecks into a tree;
Then pokes in its tongue, arrow-sharp as can be.

The long tongue of a woodpecker is attached inside its right nostril. Because of that, the bird can breathe through only its left one.

The woodpecker uses the strong point of its beak to bore a hole through the bark of a tree. It drills until it reaches the insects and grubs living inside. Its tongue then darts out from its mouth and into the hole in the tree. The bird's tongue is tipped with barbs, sharp as fishhooks. These barbs slant backward. So, when the woodpecker pulls its tongue from the tree, the barbs stick into the insects. They carry them into the bird's mouth.

Hummingbirds are so active they usually eat
Two or three times every hour, except when they sleep.

Close-up of
tongue

The hummingbird drinks nectar and eats insects. Sometimes it catches flying insects. Other times it finds them where it finds nectar – deep inside flowers. A hummer shoves its long bill and tongue into the flower. Then it uses its tongue as both a soda straw and a broom. On each side of its tongue is a groove. Through them the bird sucks up nectar. On the tip of its tongue are brushes. With them the bird sweeps insects out from inside the flower and into its bill.

One of the reasons hummingbirds must eat often is because they work so hard. When they fly and hover, they flap their wings as often as seventy times a second.

With sharp, toothy tongues as their machinery
Land snails feed at night on bits of greenery.

Radula

The tongue of a land snail has teeth growing on it. More than 14,000 of them poke up from a snail's tiny tongue. These teeth are like the bumps on a piece of sandpaper.

The tongue of a land snail is also called a *radula*. It is used to shred food from rotting plants and from fresh ones. When a snail eats, it moves its tongue in and out of its mouth. First it lays its tongue on a leaf. Then it pulls it back in. As the tongue moves over the leaf, it tears into it. Thousands of pointed tongue-teeth shred off bits of the leaf and draw them into the snail's mouth. After a land snail has finished eating, the leaf is dotted with tiny, toothy-tongue holes.

An alligator snapping turtle lives on the muddy bottom of a lake. Using its tongue as bait, it fishes for its food.

On the top of its tongue this turtle has a raised line that is shaped like a worm. Usually this ridge is white. But when the turtle is hungry, blood rushes through its tongue and colors the worm-shaped ridge red. Then the turtle opens its mouth... moves its tongue... and the ridge looks like a fat, wiggling red worm. Fish that see this "worm" swim over to eat it. When they are close enough– SNAP!– the alligator snapping turtle has caught another meal.

Fish swish eagerly toward a nice, wormy dinner.
Then, trap! They lose. A snapping turtle's the winner.

Archerfish, that sea shooter,
Has a built-in peashooter.

An archerfish lives underwater. Most of its food does not. Often it eats bugs it finds on the water's surface. Other times the only insects it sees are crawling on plants that bend over from shore. Since the archerfish can't reach them, it shoots them down.

In the roof of its mouth this fish has a groove shaped like the top half of an "O." The archer lifts its tongue to form the bottom of the "O." This tongue-tube is the archer's pea-shooter. Through it the fish shoots water pellets out from its gill chambers and up at a bug. Those pellets are hard as rocks. They can hit a bug up to six feet away. After a bug is hit, it falls from the leaf and plops down onto the water. Then the archerfish eats it up.

A whale swims along with its mouth open wide,
And scoops plants, water, shrimp, and fishes inside.

The baleen whale has no teeth. Instead it has two rows of fringed baleen hanging from the roof of its mouth. Baleen is made of the same material as are your fingernails. Its fringe hangs down like a thick curtain of brush bristles.

A baleen whale eats tiny sea animals and plants. It scoops up hundreds of pounds of them mixed with seawater before it snaps its mouth shut. Then its huge tongue rises. Like an elevator, its tongue lifts food and water into the thick fringe of baleen. The food is trapped there, but the water shoots through the fringe and out the whale's mouth. Then, with a flick of its tongue, the whale licks the food off the baleen. It gulps down that mouthful and goes scooping again.

There are so many things to be done with a tongue...

Lollipop licking,
  Leaf picking,
    Ant tricking,
      Fly sticking.
Taste food you've chewed.
Say a word that you've heard.
  Clean a kitten
    with a lick of
      a flick of
        a tongue.

The Author

Linda Hirschmann learned of the wonders of tongues with a Smithsonian scientist atop Barro Colorado in the Panama Canal. There a blue butterfly cleaned their nectar-smeared fingers with a flick of its tongue.

Her careers include teacher of mentally retarded-emotionally disturbed children, editor/writer for New York publishers, writer/public relations specialist for an antipoverty program, and manager of a twelve-room pension.

Having lived in South Carolina, New York, San Francisco, Atlanta, Boston, and Guatemala, she now makes her home in Durham, North Carolina. This is her second book for children.

The Artist

Jeni Bassett has studied at her mother's Art Workshop in Winter Park, Florida, since she was eight. Her artwork has received several awards and prizes, including a gold medal in 1978 in Scholastic Magazine's National High School Art Exhibition.

She has illustrated a number of children's books, including *Bunches and Bunches of Bunnies, Gator Pie,* and *The Great Take-Away.*